The CIA's Greatest Hits

Mark Zepezauer

Odonian Press
Tucson, Arizona

distributed by South End Press
trhough Consortium

Other titles in the Real Story series are listed on the inside back cover. You can find them at—or order them through—any good bookstore, or you can buy them directly from South End Press (800 533 8478 • www.southendpress.org • southend@southendpress.org) or from us, Odonian Press (800 REAL STORY • www.realstory.com • odonian@realstory.com). Quantity discounts are available.

Sales to the book trade are through Consortium (800 283 3572 • www.cbsd.com • consortium@cbsd.com). Real Story books are also available from wholesalers.

Title: **Charlie Winton**

Research, writing, cartoons, initial page layout and cover illustration: **Mark Zepezauer**

Rewriting, editing, inside design, final page layout and cover copy: **Arthur Naiman**

Copyediting & proofreading: **Susan McCallister, John Kadyk, Arthur Naiman**

Index: **Ty Koontz**   *Series editor:* **Arthur Naiman**

Fonts: **Basilia** *(text),* **Bookman bold italic** *(titles),* **Optima** *(headers, index, miscellaneous)*

A Real Story book from Odonian Press

Odonian Press gets its name from Ursula Le Guin's wonderful novel *The Dispossessed.* The last story in her book *The Wind's Twelve Quarters* also features the Odonians (and Odo herself).

Odonian Press donates at least 10% of its aftertax income to organizations working for social justice.

Introduction

In order to survive, nations need strong intelligence services. But the idea that the CIA is primarily an intelligence-gathering operation is itself one of the agency's greatest propaganda triumphs.

Despite its name, the Central Intelligence Agency's main purpose is—and has always been—carrying out covert operations involving economic warfare, rigged elections, assassinations and even genocide.

The CIA is also expert at distorting intelligence to justify its own goals, and this "disinformation" leads to dangerous illusions among our policymakers. But covert operations are its life's blood.

Forty-two of the CIA's biggest crimes—*far* from a complete list—are described briefly in this book. (The *Sources* section on pp. 90–91 tells you where to find more details about them.) This litany of illegal, murderous activity is enough to chill the bones of anyone who cares about liberty and justice.

As long as the CIA exists, our government can break any law it chooses in the name of national security. Anyone for whom *democracy* is more than just a word should be working to abolish the CIA. For some ideas on how to do that, send a SASE to Odonian Press at Box 66066, Tucson AZ 85728.

Mark Zepezauer

About the Author

In addition to this book, Mark Zepezauer has written *The Nixon Saga: A Pathography in Twelve Parts* and co-authored *Take the Rich Off Welfare*. He can be reached by e-mail at *comicnews@ earthlink. net.*

Contents

Hit #1: The Gehlen Org

One of the most important of all CIA operations began before the agency was even born. Many Nazi leaders realized they were going to lose World War II and started negotiating with the US behind Hitler's back about a possible future war against the USSR. In 1943, future CIA Director Allen Dulles moved to Bern, Switzerland to begin back-channel talks with these influential Nazis.

Officially, Dulles was an agent of the OSS (the Overseas Secret Service, the CIA's predecessor) but he wasn't above pursuing his own agenda with the Nazis, many of whom he had worked with before the war. Indeed, as a prominent Wall Street lawyer, Dulles had a number of clients—Standard Oil, for one—who continued doing business with the Nazis *during* the war.

So it's not surprising that when Hitler's intelligence chief for the Eastern front, General Reinhard Gehlen (GAY-len), surrendered to the US, he expected a warm reception—especially since he had buried his extensive files in a secret spot and planned to use them as a negotiating chip.

General Gehlen was whisked to Fort Hunt, Virginia, where he soon succeeded in convincing his captors that the Soviet Union was about to attack the West. The US Army and Gehlen arrived at a "gentlemen's agreement."

According to the secret treaty, his spy organization—which came to be called the Gehlen Org—would work for, and be funded by, the US until a new German government came to power. In the meantime, should Gehlen find a conflict between the interests of Germany and the US, he was free to consider German interests first.

Gehlen even made sure he got approval for this arrangement from Hitler's appointed successor, Admiral Doenitz, who was in a cushy prisoner-of-war camp for Nazi VIPs in Wiesbaden, Germany.

For almost ten years, the Gehlen Org was virtually the CIA's only source of intelligence on Eastern Europe. Then, in 1955, it evolved into the BND (the German equivalent of the CIA) which, of course, continued to cooperate with the CIA.

Gehlen was far from the only Nazi war criminal employed by the CIA. Others included Klaus Barbie ("the Butcher of Lyon"), Otto von Bolschwing (the Holocaust mastermind who worked closely with Eichmann) and, SS Colonel Otto Skorzeny (a great favorite of Hitler's). There's even evidence that Martin Bormann, Hitler's second-in-command at the end of the war, faked his own death and escaped to Latin America, where he worked with CIA-linked groups.

Hit #2: Operation Gladio

The CIA was created by the National Security Act of 1947. The ink was barely dry on it before an army of spooks began marching through the law's major loophole: the CIA could "perform such other functions and duties...as the National Security Council may from time to time direct." This deliberately vague clause opened the door to a half-century of criminal activity in the name of "national security."

One of the first duties the NSC deemed necessary was the subversion of Italian democracy...in the name of democracy, of course. Italy seemed likely to elect a leftist government in the 1948 election. To make sure Italians voted instead for the candidates Washington favored—leftover brownshirt thugs from Mussolini's party and other Nazi collaborators—millions of dollars were spent on propaganda and payoffs. It was also intimated that food aid would be cut off if the election results were inconsistent with US desires.

The US got its way in 1948 without having to resort to violence but—as was discovered in 1990—the CIA had organized a secret paramilitary army in postwar Italy, with hidden stockpiles of weapons and explosives dotting the map. Called Operation Gladio *(gladius* is Latin for *sword),* the ostensible excuse for it was laughable—the threat of a Soviet invasion. But the real purpose wasn't so funny—Operation Gladio's 15,000 troops were trained to overthrow the Italian government should it stray from the straight and narrow.

Similar secret armies were formed in France, Belgium, the Netherlands and West Germany—often directed, quite naturally, by former SS officers. They didn't just wait around for the Russians to come marching in; they assembled huge arms caches (many of which remain unaccounted for), compiled blacklists of leftists and, in France, participated in plots to assassinate President DeGaulle.

Many members of Operation Gladio were also in a shadowy organization known as P-2; it too was financed by the CIA. P-2 had connections with the Vatican and the Mafia, and eventually with an international fascist umbrella organization called the World Anti-Communist League (see Hit #32).

One of P-2's specialties was the art of provocation. Leftist organizations like the Red Brigades were infiltrated, financed and/or created, and the resulting acts of terrorism, like the assassination of Italy's premier in 1978 and the bombing of the railway station in Bologna in 1980, were blamed on the left. The goal of this "strategy of tension" was to convince Italian voters that the left was violent and dangerous—by helping make it so.

Hit #3: Iran

The history of the CIA in Iran shows that it isn't the failures of the agency we need to worry about, numerous though they are. Its successes—and Iran is one of the biggest—are far more dangerous.

The CIA did exactly what was asked of it in Iran, deposing a mildly nationalist regime that was a minor irritant to US policymakers. As a direct result, a fiercely nationalist regime came to power 26 years later, and it's proved to be a major irritant to the US ever since.

In 1951, Dr. Mohammed Mossadegh, "the most popular politician in the country," was elected Prime Minister of Iran. His major election plank was the nationalization of the only oil company operating in Iran at that time—British Petroleum. The nationalization bill was passed unanimously by the Iranian Parliament.

Though Mossadegh offered BP considerable compensation, his days were numbered from that point on. The British coordinated an international economic embargo of Iran, throwing its economy into chaos. And the CIA, at the request of the British, began spending millions of dollars on ways to get rid of Mossadegh.

The CIA's plans hinged on the young Shah of Iran, Reza Pahlavi, a timid and inexperienced figurehead. (He was a mere shadow of his father, who had led a pro-Nazi regime during World War II.) In 1953, with CIA backing, the Shah ordered Mossadegh out of office and appointed a Nazi collaborator as his successor. Demonstrators filled the streets in support of Mossadegh, and the Shah fled to Rome.

Undaunted, the CIA paid for pro-Shah street demonstrators, who seized a radio station and announced that the Shah was on his way back and that Mossadegh had been deposed. In reality, it took a nine-hour tank battle in the streets of Tehran, killing hundreds, to remove Mossadegh.

Compared to the bloodshed to follow, however, that was just a drop in the bucket. In 1976, Amnesty International concluded that the Shah's CIA-trained security force, SAVAK, had the worst human rights record on the planet, and that the number and variety of torture techniques the CIA had taught SAVAK were "beyond belief."

Inevitably, in 1979, the Iranian people overthrew the bloodstained Shah, with great bitterness and hatred toward the US for installing him and backing him all those years. The radical fundamentalist regime that rules Iran today could never have found popular support without the CIA's 1953 coup and the repression that followed.

Hit #4: Guatemala

If you ever need a reminder that the CIA was founded and run by lawyers, you won't need to look any further than the overthrow of Guatemalan democracy. The Dulles brothers were partners in the Wall Street law firm of Sullivan & Cromwell; time permitting, they also worked for the US government. With John Foster Dulles heading the State Department and Allen Dulles heading the CIA, they were the czars of Eisenhower's foreign policy, and they made sure that the interests of Sullivan & Cromwell clients weren't ignored.

In 1951, Jacobo Arbenz was elected president of Guatemala by a landslide in a free and fair election. He hoped to transform Guatemala "from a backward country with a predominantly feudal economy to a modern capitalist state." The CIA, however, weighed in heavily on the side of feudalism.

When Arbenz appropriated some unused land controlled by the Rockefeller-owned United Fruit Company (for which United Fruit was duly compensated), the company undertook an extensive PR campaign in the US, designed to paint Arbenz as a tool of the "international Communist conspiracy." John Foster Dulles, ever alert for opportunities to roll back the red menace—and to help out a valued client—convinced Ike that Arbenz must go.

Brother Allen's CIA was only too happy to take the job, which ended up costing only about $20 million. The agency sponsored a propaganda offensive and hired about 300 mercenaries who sporadically sabotaged trains and oil supplies.

Finally, in June of 1954, unmarked CIA planes staged a series of air raids on the Guatemalan capital and dropped leaflets demanding Arbenz's resignation. At the same time, CIA-run radio stations warned of the impending invasion of an occupying rebel army (actually the agency's 300 hired thugs). Considering discretion the better part of valor, Arbenz fled, leaving Guatemala in the hands of the CIA's handpicked stooge, General Castillo Armas.

The CIA has always been particularly proud of the Guatemalan operation, which inaugurated a series of bloodthirsty regimes that murdered more than 100,000 Guatemalans over the next 40 years. In retrospect, however, some CIA veterans concluded that it may have come off too easily, leading to a certain overconfidence. As one CIA officer put it, "We thought we could knock off these little brown people on the cheap."

Hit #5: MK-ULTRA

The CIA says its mind control experiments were a strictly defensive response to Chinese "brainwashing" of US POWs during the Korean War (captured US pilots were making public statements denouncing US germ warfare against civilians). Actually, US brainwashing experiments predate the CIA itself.

CIA mind control activities (also called *behavior control*) did accelerate in 1953, under a program that was exempt from the usual oversight procedures. Code-named MK-ULTRA, many of its files were destroyed by CIA Director Richard Helms (who was with it from the start) when he left office in 1973, but the surviving history is nasty enough.

MK-ULTRA spooks and shrinks tested radiation, electric shocks, electrode implants, microwaves, ultrasound and a wide range of drugs on unwitting subjects, including hundreds of prisoners at California's infamous Vacaville State Prison.

The CIA saw mind control as a way to create torture-proof couriers (by implanting memories that can only be retrieved with a prearranged signal) and programmed assassins, as in *The Manchurian Candidate*. There's evidence Sirhan was treated by a CIA-linked shrink before killing RFK (see Hit #16).

The agency also wondered if it could disorient its adversaries with mind-altering substances like LSD. It was so fascinated with LSD that, in 1953, it tried to buy up the entire world supply. For many years, the agency was the principal source of LSD in the US, both legal and otherwise (one CIA-connected dealer produced tens of millions of doses).

Before ultimately dismissing LSD as unpredictable, the CIA tested it on countless people—including its own—without their consent, provoking several suicides. One CIA germ-warfare expert hurled himself out of a tenth-story window after a "surprise" dose. It was 22 years before his family found out the real reason for his death.

The agency also rented a series of apartments, staffed them with prostitutes and watched through one-way mirrors to see the effects of various substances the prostitutes slipped to the unlucky johns. When CIA auditors found out about this (in 1963), MK-ULTRA was supposedly shut down. In fact, it was simply renamed MKSEARCH, and some of its more exotic projects were trimmed.

The CIA says all its behavior control operations ended when Helms left in 1973. If you believe that, maybe they *did* learn some useful techniques from all those brainwashing experiments. (Also see Hit #28.)

Hit #6: Zaire

When the Congo (as Zaire was then known) won its independence from Belgium in 1960, Patrice Lumumba became its first prime minister. He was a charismatic leader who enjoyed strong support in the parliament, but he was able to hold office for only two months.

A leftist, Lumumba attempted to steer a neutral course between the US and the USSR—no easy task. As Kwame Nkrumah of Ghana pointed out, it was perfectly all right for Britain and France to maintain diplomatic relations with the Soviets, but any African leader who dared to do this became an enemy of the US.

Such was the fate of Lumumba. Though the CIA "regularly bought and sold Congolese politicians," it feared that Lumumba's oratorical talents would make him a thorn in their side even if he were maneuvered out of power. So they decided it made more sense to kill him.

CIA Director Allen Dulles ordered Lumumba's assassination. (A 1975 Congressional inquiry decided that "a reasonable inference" could be drawn that this was done with Eisenhower's assent.) The agency dispatched a lethal virus to Africa, but before it could be used on Lumumba, he was deposed by Zaire's president (who had CIA backing) and fled for his life.

With the CIA's help, Lumumba was captured in December 1960 by the troops of General Joseph Mobutu, who'd assumed control of the government. Lumumba was held prisoner for over a month, interrogated, tortured, then finally shot in the head. His body was dissolved in hydrochloric acid.

Mobutu has run Zaire ever since, and the lure of the country's vast mineral resources led the CIA into a marriage of convenience with him. (The CIA station in Zaire is the largest in Africa.)

Mobutu is worth billions. Almost 40% of Zaire's national revenues accrue to him and his cronies, while the average Zairian makes $190 a year.

He hands out life sentences to student protesters for "insulting the president," tosses opposition politicians into mental hospitals, suppresses religion and the press. He's so hated by his countrymen that he once had to live in a barge in the middle of the river.

Mobutu's brutality eventually alarmed even the CIA, who backed a 1977 uprising against him. When it failed, however, the CIA and Mobutu kissed and made up. In 1992, another rebellion began and continues to vie with Mobutu for power.

Hit #7: The U-2 Incident

Toward the end of his career, President Eisenhower began to have second thoughts about the people he'd served faithfully all his life. In his farewell address to the nation, he warned of "the potential for the disastrous rise of misplaced power" inherent in the "military-industrial complex."

At least some of Ike's misgivings could be traced to the U-2 incident of eight months earlier. He'd planned a peace summit involving the leaders of the US, the USSR, Britain and France. It was to be the culmination of his "crusade for peace" and a limited nuclear test ban treaty was supposed to emerge from it.

Then, on the eve of the conference, an American U-2 spy plane landed smack in the middle of Russia. Worse, the Eisenhower administration was caught in a lie. First it claimed that an "unarmed weather research flight" had strayed into Soviet territory. Then it learned that the pilot, Francis Gary Powers, had been captured alive, thousands of miles from any border (and on May Day, no less). The Soviets were predictably incensed, and the summit was called off.

In fact, contrary to Soviet claims and press reports, the U-2 wasn't shot down—it descended and crash-landed due to a fuel shortage. This was revealed by CIA Director Allen Dulles at a secret congressional hearing (the record of which was declassified in 1975).

At the same hearing, Dulles casually remarked that he "assumed" the U-2 flight had been authorized by the president. This was highly unlikely (to say the least), since Ike had not only ordered that all such flights be curtailed in preparation for his historic summit with Khrushchev, but had also temporarily scaled back covert operations in Cuba and Tibet as a way of showing good faith.

It's much more likely that the crash of the U-2 was intended to sabotage the peace summit. In addition to fearing a lessening of tensions with the Soviet Union, US hard-liners were incensed at Ike's failure to back the CIA-inspired Hungarian uprising in 1956 (although if he had, it could have led to nuclear war).

Ike took full responsibility for the U-2 incident—it was either that or admit it had been done behind his back. But in a taped phone call to John McCone (JFK's CIA Director), Ike, working on his memoirs, groped for an explanation: "I don't want to be accusing people of having fooled me, but...."

Hit #8: The Bay of Pigs

When Cuban revolutionary Fidel Castro over-threw the US-backed Batista dictatorship in 1959, he closed down the casinos and brothels and nationalized all businesses. This deprived the Mafia—and other US-based multinationals—of a very profitable cash cow.

Vice President Nixon, who had longstanding ties with the Mob (through his best friend, Bebe Rebozo, among others), began plotting with the CIA to eliminate Castro. They did this largely behind Eisenhower's back, fully expecting that Nixon would be the next president. When JFK was elected instead, he inherited an operation—an invasion of Cuba at the Bay of Pigs—about which he had serious misgivings.

While JFK was eager to get rid of Castro, he didn't want to use US forces to do it—just Cuban exiles. The CIA hoped they could provoke an incident that would force JFK to use the US military. When he held his ground and refused, the whole invasion failed (in April 1961).

It probably wouldn't have succeeded in any case. Security for the operation was poor, as was the training given the 1500-man invasion force. A planned phony attack on the US base at Guantanamo never happened, nor did the agency's other ace in the hole—the assassination of Castro.

The CIA had hired the Mafia to kill Castro (something they both dearly desired); the hit was to occur at the same time as the invasion. Ironically, because the CIA's left hand didn't know what its right hand was doing, the Mob's hit man was almost assassinated himself. He was one of eight JFK-backed exile leaders chosen to head a post-Castro government, but Nixon had them detained during the invasion. If the invasion had succeeded, all eight would have been killed, so that Nixon-backed Cubans could take over.

To shift blame from themselves, and to embarrass JFK into more militant actions, the CIA mounted a propaganda campaign that attributed the whole Bay of Pigs failure to JFK's decision to cancel a crucial air strike. In fact, the decision had been made behind JFK's back—though he took full responsibility for it, as President Eisenhower did in a similar situation (see Hit #7).

After JFK's death, the CIA's war against Castro continued. The agency has tried to kill Castro more than two dozen times, up until at least 1987. There have also been numerous cases of CIA sabotage in Cuba, including the use of germ warfare.

As for the Cuban exiles involved in the Bay of Pigs, many have turned to organized crime and freelance terrorism (see Hit #26, for example). Others have continued to work for the CIA on covert operations. And many, of course, do both.

Hit #9: John F. Kennedy

If the CIA had nothing to do with the assassination of President John F. Kennedy, they certainly have a peculiar way of showing it, since they've undermined every investigation into JFK's murder. This is hardly surprising, given the disproportionate number of CIA connections to the case.

Take the accused "lone nut," Lee Harvey Oswald. As a Marine, he was stationed at Atsugi Air Base in Japan, one of the largest CIA stations in the world and home of the ultra-secret U-2 spy plane.

Before his transparently phony "defection" to the USSR in 1959, Oswald studied Russian in the military. In Moscow, he renounced his citizenship to a CIA officer at the US Embassy, promising to tell the Russians all he knew about the U-2. When he "changed his mind" two years later, the State Department cheerfully returned his passport and loaned him the money for his trip home.

Oswald was met in New York by a member of a CIA front group that was full of Nazis. He then moved to Dallas, where he was "befriended" by Count George de Morhenschildt, who admitted shortly before his death that he'd been assigned by the CIA to debrief Oswald on his Russian sojourn.

When Oswald moved to New Orleans in the summer of 1963, he became involved, wittingly or unwittingly, with three far-right agents of the CIA who were conspiring to assassinate JFK, ostensibly for his "betrayal" at the Bay of Pigs (see Hit #8)— Guy Banister, with whom Oswald worked while continuing to pose as a Marxist; Clay Shaw, who would later be acquitted of involvement in the JFK assassination at a trial where the prosecution tried but failed to obtain proof of his CIA status; and David Ferrie, whose Civil Air Patrol unit Oswald had joined when he was 15.

Back in Dallas that fall, Oswald was seen in the company of one "Maurice Bishop," later identified as David Atlee Phillips, who was part of a group of CIA officers that despised JFK. It included the fanatical William Harvey (who had strong links to the Mafia—he hired Johnny Rosselli to have Castro killed) and future Watergate burglar Howard Hunt, who would later lose a libel suit against a newspaper that said he was involved in the JFK assassination.

There are several possible motives for CIA involvement in the assassination: JFK's perceived "softness" on communism, the fact that he'd fired CIA Director Allen Dulles and Deputy Director Charles Cabell (brother of the mayor of Dallas), and a statement he made shortly after the Bay of Pigs, in which he promised to "splinter the CIA into a thousand pieces and scatter it to the winds."

Hit #10: Vietnam 1945–1963

Long before the US military got involved there directly, Vietnam was the CIA's war. At first they waged it on behalf of the French, who struggled for nine years, from 1945 to 1954, to recapture their one-time colony (despite the war's unpopularity with the French public).

Even with CIA mercenaries fighting alongside the French, and air support from the CIA's Air America (at the time, the largest "private" airline in the world), the effort proved to be in vain.

The 1954 Geneva Accords temporarily divided Vietnam in preparation for elections in 1956. But the US wasn't interested in elections.

In the North, CIA "psywar" expert Ed Lansdale spread the rumor that the US was planning to nuke the area. This, along with other, similar tactics, created an exodus of over one million refugees, who were ferried to the south by CIA ships and planes.

In the South, the CIA wrote a constitution for "South Vietnam" (which had never been considered a separate country before), installed Ngo Dinh Diem and gave him the job of crushing anyone who had opposed the French.

US support for Diem was based on the belief that he was the one politician in Vietnam who would never negotiate with Ho Chi Minh. When, after nine more years of futile warfare, even Diem found such negotiations desirable, he was tossed aside as casually as he'd been put in place. In November 1963, he was deposed in a CIA-sponsored coup, then assassinated.

In 1945, one US intelligence agent had described Ho Chi Minh as the "strongest and perhaps the ablest figure in Indochina, and…any suggested solution which excludes him is…of uncertain outcome." Unfortunately, such insights were ignored in Washington as the Cold War solidified.

Hit #11: Dominican Republic

Rafael Trujillo took power in the Dominican Republic in a 1930 *coup d'etat* and received enthusiastic backing from Washington for most of the next 30 years. His methods for suppressing dissent were sickeningly familiar—torture and mass murder. The US raised no objections, and Trujillo returned the favor by becoming a totally reliable supporter of US policies in the UN.

As often happens with such tyrants, however, he got too greedy. His personal business holdings grew until he controlled some three-fifths of the Dominican economy, which threatened the "favorable investment climate" that client states are set up for in the first place.

Also, when it started to look like Castro's revolutionary army would take over Cuba, the US began to worry that Trujillo's excesses might inspire a similar revolution. For whatever reasons, the CIA began plotting Trujillo's assassination in 1958.

Trujillo's life came to an abrupt end in May 1961, and while proper deniability was maintained in Washington, this is one of the best-documented CIA assassination plots (according to the 1975 Church Committee). The US attempted to maintain the corrupt essence of the Trujillo regime without Trujillo, but the 1962 elections brought a physician named Juan Bosch to power.

Bosch was anti-Communist and pro-business but, foolish man, he was dedicated to establishing a "decent democratic regime" through land reform, low-rent housing and public works projects. He was deposed by a CIA-backed coup after only seven months in office. When a popular countercoup tried to restore Bosch to power in 1965, the US invaded the island and installed a series of murderous regimes which have maintained a favorable investment climate ever since.

While he never lived long enough to see it enshrined as the "JFK Doctrine," President Kennedy once offered a fairly clear-cut rationale for US interventions abroad. Referring to the Dominican Republic, he said, "there are three possibilities...a decent democratic regime, a continuation of the Trujillo regime, or a Castro regime [by which he meant Bosch]. We ought to aim at the first, but we really can't renounce the second until we are sure that we can avoid the third."

In practice, we've hardly ever used the first option. Virtually all of our client states are similar to the Trujillo regime—and to the regimes we replaced him with.

Hit #12: Malcolm X

In the last years of his life, Malcolm X did a number of things that angered the CIA. He stated many times that he believed the CIA was behind the Lumumba assassination (it was—see Hit #6). He held widely publicized meetings with anti-imperialist Third World leaders, many of whom were later overthrown or killed in CIA-backed operations. And he planned to ask the UN to officially declare American blacks an oppressed minority, which would be a major embarrassment to the US. (Ten years earlier, the CIA had ruined the career of black leader Paul Robeson over the same threat.)

But another development scared the the government even more—Malcolm, no longer a separatist, was forging alliances with more moderate black leaders. If he'd lived just a week longer, he would have had his first cooperative meeting with Martin Luther King. Soon after, he would have gone to Algeria for a summit meeting of nonwhite resistance movements from all over the world.

The FBI and the CIA had been spying on Malcolm for years (in a coordinated effort), and both the Nation of Islam and Malcolm's splinter group, the OAAU (he split from the Nation of Islam a year before his death), were heavily infiltrated by government agents. In fact, one of Malcolm's bodyguards the night he was slain was working for the New York Police Department's intelligence unit; he left the scene shortly before the shooting started.

Malcolm had expressed doubts to his biographer that the Nation of Islam could be behind all the things that happened to him in the year before he was killed. "I know what they can do and what they can't do," he'd said, "and they can't do some of the stuff recently going on."

Malcolm was shot to death by five gunmen while giving a speech in Harlem in February 1965. All but one of the assassins escaped. The three men eventually charged with the murder were all members of the Nation of Islam. In 1979, one of them revealed that the conspiracy to kill Malcolm had included one of the highest-ranking FBI infiltrators in the Nation of Islam.

With Malcolm dead, the coalition between the more radical and the more moderate wings of the black liberation movement never came to pass. His resolution regarding the oppression of American blacks reached the floor of the UN, but without Malcolm's charisma to draw attention to it, it was ignored.

Hit #13: Indonesia

Some people justify the CIA's crimes by saying that we faced a brutal and ruthless enemy in the Cold War, and winning was of paramount importance. The problem with that argument is that no one could have been more brutal and ruthless than the allies we embraced. There's no clearer illustration of this than Indonesia, the fourth most populous nation in the world.

From 1945 to 1965, Sukarno was president of Indonesia. A star among Third World leaders, active in the nonaligned, anti-imperialist movement, he'd long been a thorn in the side of the US. Worse yet, the Communist party was part of his governing coalition. The CIA had backed a failed uprising against him (in 1958), had tried to assassinate him and had even attempted to embarrass him by making a porno film starring a Sukarno look-alike!

In 1965, they finally scored. The Indonesian military, trained and backed by the US, provoked a leftist coup against its leader, General Suharto. When the coup failed, the military used it as an excuse to depose Sukarno and replace him with Suharto. (According to diplomatic documents, the coup was a setup to justify the military takeover.)

What followed (as depicted in the film *The Year of Living Dangerously*) is almost beyond belief. In just a few weeks, between five hundred thousand and a million Indonesians were put to death, many in a grisly fashion. (But don't worry—the Suharto regime assures us they were all Communists.) It was later learned that the death squads had been working from hit lists provided by the US State Department (the usual cover for CIA agents).

The 1965 massacre was only the beginning for Indonesia's new military regime. In 1975, its army invaded the tiny nation of East Timor, a former Portuguese colony which has the bad luck to own significant oil reserves.

Since then, *between a quarter and a third* of East Timor's inhabitants, from all ethnic and religious groups, have been slaughtered by the Indonesian military, with arms largely supplied and paid for by the US.

On a per-capita basis, East Timor is the greatest genocide since the Holocaust. Combined with the 1965 killings and other Indonesian atrocities, it puts Suharto in the first rank of twentieth-century mass murderers, right up there with Hitler, Stalin, the Turks who massacred the Armenians in 1915 and the generals who run Guatemala (see Hit #4).

Hit #14: Greece

In April 1967, a Greek election campaign was about to begin. The candidate favored to win the election was George Papandreou, a staunch anti-communist. His son Andreas was a bit more left-wing, an admirer of subversives like Hubert Humphrey and Adlai Stevenson. Both the Papandreous, however, were a bit too independent for US policymakers.

Andreas Papandreou had mused publicly about steering a more neutral course for Greece in the Cold War. He also had some misgivings—correct ones, as it turned out—about the autocratic nature of certain elements in the Greek military.

George Papandreou had previously served as prime minister, but had been removed from power in 1965 by the king, with the assistance of the CIA. Like his son, he showed signs of less than complete subservience to US interests.

Two days before the election campaign was to begin, a group of colonels overthrew the government and established military rule. The leader of the coup had been on the CIA payroll for the previous fifteen years.

For the next six years, martial law held sway in the birthplace of democracy. Widespread censorship, routine use of torture, brutal beatings and killings by the government became standard. Among the offenses deemed worthy of torture was possession of leaflets critical of the government. While being tortured, victims were taunted that they were beyond all help, since the colonels were supported by the power of the United States.

The official justification for the coup and the hideous repression that followed was that they were necessary to save the nation from a communist takeover. The Papandreous weren't communists, of course, but they were something much more dangerous—committed, independent nationalists.

The US attitude toward that breed is made clear by the following quote: When the Greek ambassador objected to President Johnson's plan for settling a dispute concerning Cyprus, LBJ told him, "Fuck your parliament and your constitution. America is an elephant. Cyprus is a flea. Greece is a flea. If these two fleas continue itching the elephant, they may just get whacked by the elephant's trunk, whacked good....If your prime minister gives me talk about democracy, parliament and constitutions, he, his parliament and his constitution may not last very long."

Hit #15: Martin Luther King, Jr.

After pleading guilty to assassinating Martin Luther King, Jr. and being sentenced to 99 years, James Earl Ray said he was coerced into the plea by his Mob-connected lawyer. He insists he was framed for the King murder by a mysterious man named Raoul, for whom he had been working in the spring of 1968, just before the assassination.

Certainly there's something fishy about the idea that Ray acted alone. He eluded a massive, three-and-a-half-month, international manhunt, escaping to Europe by way of Canada. This required *a lot* more cunning and financial resources than an incompetent, smalltime thief and drifter like Ray could muster.

But the fishiest thing about Ray's escape was the four very detailed and precise aliases he used. All were the names of men who lived in the same section of Toronto (where Ray had never been) and each man bore a strong physical resemblance to Ray, right down to their scars. In at least one case, Ray also seems to have had access to information that could only have come from the alias' military records.

In 1989, a convicted murderer named Jules Kimble shed some light on all this. He claimed he'd been part of a conspiracy to kill King that included members of the CIA, the FBI and the Mafia.

Jules Kimble says he introduced Ray to a CIA identities expert in Montreal in 1967, who provided Ray with the aliases he used as a fugitive. Investigators discovered that a CIA identities expert was indeed working in Montreal at that time. His name? Raoul Miora.

This alone ought be enough to reopen the case, but there's more to Kimble's story. He says that after meeting with Raoul, he took Ray to a CIA training camp, and later to Memphis, where a seven-man hit squad assassinated King.

Kimble claims Ray was part of the conspiracy, but was framed for the murder by means of a bundle of his belongings which was left at the scene of the crime. In the bundle was the supposed murder weapon with Ray's prints on it.

Kimble was connected with both Mob and intelligence figures during the period in question, including David Ferrie, a prime suspect in the JFK assassination (Hit #9). And the official account of Ray's supposed activities has more holes in it than a piece of cheesecloth (see the *Sources* on page 90 for more details).

Hit #16: Robert Kennedy

Hundreds of books have been written about whether there was a conspiracy in the JFK assassination. In the murder of his brother, Senator Robert Kennedy, the case for conspiracy can be summed up in one sentence: The Los Angeles coroner's report states that RFK was killed by a *point-blank shot from behind,* while everyone agrees that Sirhan Sirhan, the convicted assassin, was *at least three feet in front of him.*

There's a lot of evidence of CIA involvement in the RFK assassination. For one thing, despite the clear fact that there had to be a second gunman, the Los Angeles Police Department's special task force investigating the case bent over backwards to prove Sirhan was the lone assassin. Witnesses were intimidated, evidence was destroyed and plausible suspects weren't questioned.

Two key members of the task force had long-standing ties to the CIA, and were especially zealous about browbeating witnesses whose testimony suggested a conspiracy. They got very upset when anyone mentioned the famous "girl in the polka-dot dress" (who was seen fleeing the scene of the crime shouting, "We shot him!") and made sure that any mention of her was eliminated from the testimony.

Another obvious suspect who was barely investigated is the Rev. Jerry Owen, who was seen with Sirhan in the days before the murder. Owen admitted knowing Mafia courier Edgar Bradley, who also was present at the JFK assassination (Hit #9). Bradley, who was actually arrested in Dealey Plaza, then released without being charged, appears to be linked to other key figures in the JFK case.

Then there's the late Dr. William Bryan, Jr, a hypnosis expert involved with the CIA's mind control experiments (see Hit #5). Bryan liked to brag of the famous subjects he had worked on—including, reportedly, Sirhan, who is extraordinarily susceptible to hypnosis. The name of another famous Bryan patient, the Boston Strangler, inexplicably turns up in Sirhan's notebooks.

Sirhan claims to have no memory of shooting at RFK or writing in his notebooks, and he appears to be telling the truth. Witnesses to the crime report that he seemed to be in some sort of trance.

More attention should also be focused on Thane Cesar, a security guard with right-wing, Mob and CIA connections who was standing directly behind RFK and who admits that he drew his gun.

Finally, one-time CIA man Robert Morrow wrote a book alleging that an agent of Iran's SAVAK (see Hit #3) was hired to kill RFK.

Hit #17: Chile

In 1973, the CIA destroyed the oldest functioning democracy in South America. Twenty years later, the agency is still trying to deny its involvement.

The CIA intervened massively in Chile's 1958 and 1964 elections. In 1970, its fears were realized—the socialist candidate, a physician named Salvador Allende, was elected president.

Horrified, President Nixon ordered the CIA to prevent Allende's inauguration. The agency did its best to promote a military coup, but the Chilean military's long history of respect for the democratic process made this virtually impossible. One of the main impediments was the Chilean army's chief of staff, General Rene Schneider, so the CIA plotted with fanatics in the military to assassinate him. The killing backfired, solidifying support for Allende, who took office as scheduled.

That approach having failed, the CIA was ordered to create a "coup climate." ("Make the economy scream," President Nixon told CIA Director Helms.) CIA-backed acts of sabotage and terror multiplied. The agency trained members of the fascist organization Patria y Libertad (PyL) in guerrilla warfare and bombing, and they were soon waging a campaign of arson.

The CIA also sponsored demonstrations and strikes, funded by ITT and other US corporations with Chilean holdings. CIA-linked media, including the country's largest newspaper, fanned the flames of crisis. The military's patriotism was gradually eroded by endless stories about Marxist "atrocities" like castration and cannibalism, and rumors that the military would be purged or "destroyed" and Soviet bases set up.

When the coup finally came, in September 1973, it was led by the most extreme fascist members of the military, and it was unrelenting in its ferocity. Allende was assassinated (some CIA apologists maintain he committed suicide—by shooting himself with a machine gun!). Several cabinet ministers were also assassinated, the universities were put under military control, opposition parties were banned and thousands of Chileans were tortured and killed, many fingered as "radicals" by lists provided by the CIA.

Under the military junta headed by General Pinochet, torture of dissidents became routine, particularly at a gruesome prison called Colonia Dignidad. It drew expatriate Nazis from all over South America, one of whom told a victim that the work of the Nazi death camps was being continued there.

No wonder the CIA tries to deny it was involved in the Chilean coup. It turned a democratic, peaceloving nation into a slaughterhouse.

Hit #18: Vietnam 1964–1975

Following the deaths of JFK (Hit #9) and Ngo Dinh Diem (see Hit #10), it was only a matter of time before US combat troops became involved in Vietnam. Within days of the JFK assassination in November 1963, President Johnson had reversed JFK's plan to withdraw US personnel by the end of 1965. As LBJ told one impatient general, "Just get me elected; you can have your damn war."

In August 1964, the CIA and related military intelligence agencies helped fabricate a phony Vietnamese attack in the Gulf of Tonkin off North Vietnam. This supposed act of North Vietnamese aggression was used as the basis for escalating US involvement.

In March 1965, US troops began pouring into Vietnam. Nine years of backing the French, another nine years of backing Diem and two more years of CIA operations had failed. From this point on, the US Army took over the war effort.

Since the Vietnamese people overwhelmingly supported their own National Liberation Front (the NLF, or "Viet Cong" as we called it), the Army began destroying villages, herding people into internment camps, weeding out the leaders and turning the countryside into a "free-fire zone" (in other words, shoot anything that moves).

The CIA still had a role to play, however. Called Operation Phoenix, it was an assassination program plain and simple. The idea was to cripple the NLF by killing influential people like mayors, teachers, doctors, tax collectors—anyone who aided the functioning of the NLF's parallel government in the South.

Many of the "suspects" were tortured and some were tossed from helicopters during interrogation. William Colby, the CIA official in charge of Phoenix (he later became director of the CIA), insisted this was all part of "military necessity" — though he admitted to Congress that he really had no idea how many of the 20,000 killed were Viet Cong and how many were "loyal" Vietnamese.

Colby's confusion was understandable, since Phoenix was a joint operation between the US and the South Vietnamese, who used it as a means of extortion, a protection racket and a way to settle vendettas. Significantly, the South Vietnamese estimated the Operation Phoenix death toll at closer to 40,000. Whatever the exact number, there's no question the killings were necessary—after all, we were trying to prevent a bloodbath.

Hit #19: Laos

Between 1957 and 1965, Laotian governments came and went at a frantic pace, with the CIA sponsoring at least one coup a year. The problem was a leftist group called the Pathet Lao which kept getting enough votes to be included in coalition governments.

If the Pathet Lao or other leftists were voted into office, there'd either be a right-wing coup or the legislature would be dissolved, with future elections canceled if possible. If there was an election, the CIA would stuff ballot boxes, run propaganda campaigns and bribe legislators to try to get their candidates elected.

But the CIA didn't rely primarily on such namby-pamby techniques. Starting in the late 1950s, they recruited a mercenary force of some 40,000 men to attack Pathet Lao forces. Known as the Armée Clandestine ("secret army"), about half its members were from Thailand; the rest came from Taiwan, South Korea and other US client states. Despite the size of the Armée Clandestine, the Pathet Lao had enough support in the countryside to withstand it.

By 1964, after another CIA coup succeeded in installing a right-wing puppet, the Pathet Lao was completely frozen out of the electoral process. They'd begun receiving aid from the neighboring North Vietnamese, who were concerned about CIA-backed sabotage and assassination teams operating from Laotian territory. When the Pathet Lao made significant advances, the US military got directly—although secretly—involved.

From 1965 to 1973, the US dropped over *two million tons* of bombs on Laos, far more than all sides dropped in World War II. The bombing was so ferocious that over a quarter of the population became refugees, with many people living in caves for years at a time.

Since this CIA-run war in Laos was "secret," it only received a fraction of the attention given to the war in Vietnam. The secrecy proved unfortunate for many of the US soldiers involved.

If killed, they were listed as casualties of the Vietnam war. But when the Pathet Lao finally took power in 1975, no prisoner exchange treaty was signed, because we couldn't admit we'd been running a secret war in Laos.

Many of the Americans known to have been captured alive in Laos were involved in drug trafficking with the Armée Clandestine. If any are still alive, the CIA would have a considerable interest in denying their existence.

Hit #20: Cambodia

In 1955, when CIA intervention in Cambodia began, there was no communist threat to rationalize it. Sandwiched as he was between two US client states, Thailand and South Vietnam, Prince Norodom Sihanouk, the popular sovereign of Cambodia, had one overriding goal—to keep his country from becoming involved in the Vietnam War. To that end, he stuck tenaciously to a policy of neutralism from 1955 to 1970, accepting aid from both communist and capitalist states but criticizing each on occasion.

Sihanouk dismissed as fraudulent CIA documents that predicted imminent Communist aggression against him, but the plots and coup attempts by US-backed factions were all too real. In his memoir, *My War with the CIA,* Sihanouk alleges at least two assassination plots against him. There were also numerous incursions by Thai, South Vietnamese and US troops, a 1958 CIA-backed coup attempt and countless "accidental" bombing runs into Cambodian territory. Sihanouk's unwillingness to join the crusade against Communism made him the CIA's enemy.

Perhaps the final straw was when Sihanouk denounced US military incursions into Cambodia at a major press conference (dutifully, the US media barely mentioned his charges). In March 1970, Sihanouk was deposed by a CIA puppet named Lon Nol, who immediately began committing Cambodian troops to the war in Vietnam.

With Sihanouk out of the way, war quickly engulfed Cambodia. US bombing intensified near the Vietnamese border, driving North Vietnamese and NLF troops deeper into Cambodia (see Hit

#18 for more on the war in Vietnam). From 1969 to 1975, US bombing killed 600,000 Cambodians and created a full-scale famine.

Not surprisingly, forces opposed to Lon Nol's regime grew rapidly. In 1975, one of them, the Communist Khmer Rouge, took power (before Lon Nol, they'd been a tiny, marginal group).

As depicted in the film *The Killing Fields,* the Khmer Rouge carried out many atrocities, executing probably between 100,000 and 350,000 people. For propaganda purposes, Western reporters inflated the total by adding famine deaths to it.

The Khmer Rouge's hideous crimes didn't prevent the CIA from supporting it after Vietnam invaded Cambodia in 1979, and for many years thereafter. As the Arabs say, "the enemy of my enemy is my friend."

Hit #21: Operation CHAOS

In theory, the CIA's charter prohibits it from engaging in domestic operations. In practice, that's taken about as seriously as Frank Sinatra's periodic announcements that he's retiring from show biz.

The CIA explains its massive presence on US campuses by saying that so many foreign students attend US universities, it would be a shame not to try to recruit them. The Domestic Contacts Division is needed to glean information from US tourists and businessmen returning from abroad. Then there's the Domestic Operations Division, which handles foreign interventions on US soil, like breaking into foreign embassies.

In order to do all that, the CIA has had to set up the same sort of network of phony businesses and front organizations it uses overseas. But other than that, it claims it never operates domestically.

Unfortunately, that's not true. From 1959 to at least 1974, the CIA used its domestic organizations to spy on thousands of US citizens whose only crime was disagreeing with their government's policies.

This picked up speed when J. Edgar Hoover told President Johnson that nobody would be protesting his Vietnam war policies unless they were being directed to do so by some foreign power. Johnson ordered the CIA to investigate.

In response, the CIA vastly expanded its campus surveillance program and stepped up its liaisons with local police departments. It trained special intelligence units in major cities to carry out "black bag" jobs (break-ins, wiretaps, etc.) against US "radicals."

In 1968, the CIA's various domestic programs were consolidated and expanded under the name Operation CHAOS. When Richard Nixon became president the following year, his administration drafted the Huston Plan, which called for even greater operations against "subversives," including wiretapping, break-ins, mail-opening, no-knock searches and "selective assassinations." Bureaucratic infighting tabled the plan, but much of it was implemented in other forms, not only by the CIA but also by the FBI and the Secret Service.

With the revelation of CIA and White House complicity in the Watergate break-in (Hit #23), light began to shine on Operation CHAOS. After a period of "reform," much of CHAOS's work was privatized, and right-wing groups and "former" CIA agents now provide the bulk of the CIA's domestic intelligence.

Hit #22: Drug Trafficking

Even before the CIA was officially founded, it was intertwined with major drug-trafficking organizations—its parent organization, the OSS, cooperated with the Mafia during World War II. After the war, one of the first covert operations of the new CIA was to break the strength of left-wing labor unions in southern France. To do this, the CIA cemented an ongoing tie to the Corsican Mafia, then the biggest heroin traffickers in the world.

By the early 1960s, much of the world's heroin production had shifted to Southeast Asia, due to another major CIA operation. The agency had trained Nationalist Chinese forces to invade Communist China; when that operation failed, they settled in northeastern Burma and became the world's largest opium producers (mainly by terrorizing the local villagers into growing it for them). This area, known as the Golden Triangle, continues to lead the world in opium production.

Meanwhile, as the US moved into Indochina (see Hits #18–20), the existing opium trade there gradually became integrated into other US operations. While President Nixon, full of law-and-order rhetoric, made a great show of busting the famous "French connection," his allies in the Florida Mafia moved into Vietnam. By 1970, the US was flooded with pure Asian heroin, some of it smuggled home inside the corpses of US soldiers.

In Laos, the CIA was running a 40,000-man mercenary army (see Hit #19). It included many Hmong tribespeople, who were longtime opium farmers. The CIA airline, Air America, ran weapons to the army and brought the Hmong's crop back out to market. Some of the massive profits from the operations were laundered by CIA agent Michael Hand through an Australian bank he founded (see Hit #38) and were used to finance other CIA operations behind Congress' back.

Many veterans of CIA drug operations in Asia went on to star in the agency's secret wars in Central America in the 1980s (see Hits #32–34 & #39), where the above pattern was repeated. The Nicaraguan contras were partially funded by cocaine operations, smuggled to and from the US on customs-free supply flights. CIA assets in Honduras, Costa Rica, El Salvador and Panama helped facilitate the trade.

In the CIA's secret war in Afghanistan (Hit #36), the Afghan rebels and their Pakistani hosts also partly financed themselves with heroin profits. Much of their product ended up, once again, in the veins of US addicts.

Hit #23: Watergate

No one knows exactly why the team of freelance spooks called the "plumbers" (because they were hired to fix leaks) broke into the Watergate office complex in Washington DC on the night of June 17, 1972. Most theories center on Nixon's need to find out what kind of blackmail the Democrats had on him. Others say it was a case of Nixon and the CIA trying to blackmail each other, and there are several intriguing CIA-Watergate connections.

The Watergate break-in was so badly mishandled that some people think it was deliberately botched. The man doing the botching was James McCord, onetime chief of security for the CIA. He twice placed masking tape on a doorjamb in a way the Watergate guard couldn't miss. And it was McCord who wrote a letter to a federal judge, just as the affair was about to be swept under the rug, warning that "higher-ups" were covering up their involvement in Watergate.

One of the plumbers who went to jail, Howard Hunt—a longtime CIA officer and a player in the JFK assassination (see Hit #9)—successfully blackmailed Nixon for over one million dollars, but he may have pushed his luck too far. His wife, carrying a suitcase full of cash, was killed in a mysterious plane crash. Convincing evidence suggests the flight had been deliberately sabotaged.

Later, another CIA man, Alexander Butterfield, let slip to the Senate Watergate Committee that the President was in the habit of taping his Oval Office conversations, providing the final nail for Nixon's coffin. Butterfield, on leave from the CIA, had requested assignment to the White House.

Washington Post reporter Bob Woodward received dirt on Watergate from a secret source he called Deep Throat, a man clearly familiar with the intelligence community. Woodward himself had been a top-security briefer for the Office of Naval Intelligence and both his editor, Ben Bradlee, and *Post* publisher Katherine Graham's late husband had also worked for the CIA.

Nixon told his chief of staff, Bob Haldeman, to call the CIA off its Watergate investigation because it could "blow the whole Bay of Pigs thing." When Haldeman took this message to CIA Director Richard Helms, Helms erupted. "The Bay of Pigs had nothing to do with this!" he shouted.

What were they talking about? According to Haldeman, "the Bay of Pigs" was Nixon's coded way of referring to the assassination of JFK.

Hit #24: The Mighty Wurlitzer

Deputy Director Frank Wisner proudly referred to the CIA's worldwide propaganda machine as "the mighty Wurlitzer." And indeed, the agency's skill at murdering people is matched only by its ability to murder the truth.

The CIA has published literally hundreds of books that spread its party line on the Cold War. It was particularly proud of *The Penikovsky Papers,* supposedly the memoirs of a KGB defector but actually completely ghostwritten by CIA scribes. A bit more embarrassing was Claire Sterling's *The Octopus,* which advanced the now-discredited theory that the Russians were behind the 1981 attempt on the life of Pope John Paul II. Even the popular *Fodor's Travel Guides* started as a CIA front.

The CIA also owns dozens of newspapers and magazines the world over. These not only provide cover for their agents but allow them to plant misinformation that regularly makes it back to the US through the wire services. The CIA has even placed agents on guard at the wire services, to prevent inconvenient facts from being disseminated.

In 1977, famed Watergate journalist Carl Bernstein revealed that over 400 US journalists had been employed by the CIA. These ranged from freelancers who were paid for regular debriefings, to actual CIA officers who worked under deep cover. Nearly every major US news organization has had spooks on the payroll, usually with the cooperation of top management.

The three most valuable media assets the CIA could count on were William Paley's CBS, Arthur Sulzberger's *New York Times* and Henry Luce's *Time/Life* empire. All three bent over backwards promoting the picture of Oswald as a lone nut in the JFK assassination (Hit #9).

Among prominent journalists who've worked knowingly with the CIA are *National Review* founder William F. Buckley, PBS interviewer Bill Moyers, the late columnist Stewart Alsop, former *Washington Post* editor Ben Bradlee and *Ms.* magazine founder Gloria Steinem.

Bernstein's landmark article on the CIA and the media told of the agency's frantic efforts to limit Congressional inquiry into the matter, with claims that "some of the biggest names in journalism could get smeared." And while the CIA director at the time, George Bush, made a not-too-convincing show of discontinuing the agency's manipulation of the media, it's clear that the CIA regards the space between your ears as one of its most important battlefields.

Hit #25: Angola

The Angolan intervention is a strong candidate for the most pointless CIA operation ever. Certainly the ratio of blood spilled to goals achieved—to the extent that those goals can even be determined—makes it one of the agency's biggest fiascos.

In 1975, the collapse of the Portuguese empire left its African colony of Angola with three groups struggling for power. Each had at various times flirted with both capitalism and Marxism, and each had taken aid from both East and West. Zaire (a US ally) backed one faction, the Soviets backed another (the MPLA) and the CIA ended up backing the third, Jonas Savimbi's UNITA.

The main reason for the CIA's involvement in Angola was Henry Kissinger's determination to start another war as soon as possible after the fall of Saigon, to show the world how tough we were. We said we were worried about oil—even though there isn't much of it in Angola, and the MPLA, which has controlled the oil since 1975, has continued to sell it to the West throughout the war. Another absurd excuse: Angola is close to "shipping lanes" (just like every other coastal nation on earth).

No diplomatic option was ever pursued by Kissinger. Instead, the CIA put untold amounts of blood and treasure behind Savimbi—a brutal, bloodthirsty autocrat. Our apparent determination to turn Angola into a Cold War battlefield brought in South African troops, who supported Savimbi, and—in response—Cuban troops, who supported the MPLA with great success.

South Africa's involvement was part of its efforts to destabilize all of its neighbors, in order to delay the inevitable ascension of its black majority to power. Since they were supporting our faction, this caused considerable damage to US relations with black Africa.

FINE ANGOLAN HORSES —TAKE YOUR PICK

After $40 million and thousands of dead, Congress—in a rare display of principle—cut off funds for the Angolan war in 1976, the first time it had ever voted to shut down a CIA operation. Unfortunately, the CIA managed to sustain the killing off-the-books until Reagan took office in 1981. Millions more dollars and thousands more lives were then wasted until, in 1990, the ongoing Angolan stalemate at last resulted in an election.

When Savimbi lost overwhelmingly to the MPLA, he cranked the war right back up again, initially with further CIA funding. Finally, in 1993, the US distanced itself from Savimbi and recognized the MPLA government, but the war still continues. So far, more than 300,000 Angolans have died, 80,000 are crippled, 50,000 orphaned, and the damage to property exceeds $50 billion.

Hit #26: Orlando Letelier

"Are you the wife of Orlando Letelier?" asked the anonymous caller. "Yes," she answered. "No," the caller said, " you are his widow."

A week later, on September 21, 1976, the exiled Chilean diplomat and prominent critic of the CIA-backed Pinochet regime (see Hit #17) was torn to pieces by a car bomb on the streets of Washington DC. Also killed was Letelier's American aide, Ronni Moffit. Her husband, blown clear of the car, immediately began shouting that Chilean fascists were responsible for the atrocity.

He was right, but those fascists had powerful allies in Washington. An FBI informant knew of the plot to assassinate Letelier before the fact but the FBI did nothing to protect him. After the bombing, CIA Director George Bush told the FBI that there'd been no Chilean involvement whatever. The CIA was certain of this, he said, because it had many reliable sources inside the Chilean secret police, DINA.

Actually, the CIA had known that a DINA hit squad was in the US and headed for Washington. After the bombing, the agency purged its files of photos of the assassins. The CIA and DINA then began planting stories in the press suggesting that Letelier had been killed by leftists seeking to make a martyr of him.

The FBI figured out the identities of Letelier's assassins within weeks, but didn't charge them until the CIA's cover-up unraveled several years later. The unraveling began a month after the killing, when a Cuban airliner was bombed, killing 73 passengers. That bombing was done by a violent group of CIA-linked Cuban exiles who were connected with the Bay of Pigs and the JFK assassination (Hits #8 & #9) and who went on to do similar things in El Salvador and Nicaragua (Hits #32 & #33).

Investigators into the airliner bombing discovered that both it and the Letelier/Moffit killings were planned at the same meeting, which was organized by a man with longtime CIA connections and was attended by other FBI and CIA men.

Apologists argue that no one can prove that Letelier's convicted assassins, "former" CIA agent Michael Townley and two Cuban exiles, were acting under agency orders. But if they weren't, why did the CIA immediately begin covering up for them?

This case is so complex that, in 1991, the Chilean Supreme Court (post-Pinochet) asked George Bush if he'd mind submitting to questioning. You'd better believe he minded.

Hit #27: Team B

In 1949, an influential senator told President Truman that if he wanted to justify massive Cold War military spending, he'd have to "scare the hell out of the American people." That's a mission the CIA has always taken to heart. From the very beginning, it's overestimated Soviet military strength, in part because of its dependence on the Gehlen Org (see Hit #1) for Eastern Bloc intelligence.

There were many subtle ways of cooking the books. One was to estimate Soviet spending as though their soldiers were paid as much as US personnel, though in fact they received far less. Another was to release misleading data on how much larger Soviet missiles were than ours (which actually meant they were more primitive) or to compare missile capabilities based on the Soviets' greater "throw weight" (which was needed to push their huge, inaccurate missiles). Some reports pretended that the entire Soviet military was poised to invade Europe, when much of it was actually defending the Chinese border.

There was, in fact, a group of CIA analysts who had a fairly sophisticated understanding of the actual capabilities of (and factions within) the USSR, but they were regarded as dangerous pinkos by the hawks within the agency. Some of these hawks served on the Committee on the Present Danger (CPD), a private group that lobbied for massive hikes in military spending and that backed Ronald Reagan for president in 1976.

When George Bush (who'd been a CIA asset since the late 1950s) became CIA director in 1975, one of his duties was to oversee a project called Team B. This was an offering from President Ford to the CPD and other right-wingers who argued that CIA analysts were underestimating Soviet military strength, and who wanted a second opinion.

The CIA analysts regarded Bush's backing of Team B to rewrite their data as a betrayal, but Reagan rewarded Bush by making him his running mate in 1980. Once elected, Reagan named every one of the Team B members to sensitive military posts, and jacked up the Pentagon budget.

When Bush became president in 1989, he chose as his CIA director Robert Gates, who'd been the leader of the pro-Team B faction in the CIA during Bush's tenure as director. Gates had spent the Reagan years providing seriously distorted intelligence estimates of Soviet strength, which may be why the CIA was so woefully unprepared to anticipate the collapse of the USSR.

Hit #28: Jonestown

There's lots of evidence that the mass murder at Jonestown, Guyana in 1978 was the culmination of a massive and barbarous CIA behavior control experiment. And mass murder is what it was—not mass suicide, as widely reported. The Guyanese coroner's report states that the 913 victims didn't drink the mythical cyanide-laced Kool-Aid—there was no trace of cyanide poisoning in their bodies. 80–90% of the victims had been injected with lethal agents, while the rest were shot. The coroner concluded that only two had committed suicide.

Cult leader Jim Jones had longstanding ties to the CIA, stretching back to his boyhood friendship with the notorious CIA torture expert Dan Mitrione. Mitrione regarded torture as an art form and, while instructing security forces in Brazil and Uruguay, he had beggars kidnapped so he could practice on them. Mitrione's old pal Jones was in Brazil at the same time, and he made frequent trips to Belo Horizonte, site of the local CIA headquarters.

Jones returned from Brazil to found the People's Temple in Ukiah, California. Early on he engaged in shocking abuses of his cult members. He also used them to infiltrate the organizations of liberal politicians, getting out the vote and making them beholden to him for favors. San Francisco Mayor George Moscone and Supervisor Harvey Milk, who were assassinated a week after Jonestown, both owed political favors to Jones. So did the district attorney whose lenient prosecution of the assassin let him get off with only a token sentence.

When reports of murders tied to the People's Temple began to surface, Jones fled with his flock to Guyana, whose prime minister owed his job to a 1964 CIA coup. Jones was in close touch with CIA agents at the US Embassy, at least one of whom was at Jonestown at the time of the massacre.

Survivors report that Jonestown was a virtual concentration camp where the mostly black cultists worked like slaves. They were beaten, tortured, raped and given massive doses of both verbal indoctrination and drugs. Many of the mind-altering substances used in the MK-ULTRA program (see Hit #5) were found at Jonestown, in amounts sufficient to subdue a city of 200,000.

The end came when Rep. Leo Ryan, a key congressional opponent of the CIA, arrived to investigate and was assassinated by Jones' followers. Then the mass killings began, though Jones' wealthy white lieutenants escaped free from harm. Millions in cash were found at the site, but the bulk of Jones' fortune, estimated at $2 billion, disappeared into secret bank accounts. As for Jones himself, photographs of what are supposed to be his body don't show his tattoos.

Hit #29: The October Surprise

When Ronald Reagan was running for president against Jimmy Carter in 1980, 52 American hostages were being held in Iran. The Reagan/Bush campaign feared that if the hostages were released before the November election, the resulting "October surprise" might help Carter win.

According to former Iranian President Bani-Sadr, Reagan officials met with the Iranians in Paris in October 1980 and gave them $40 million in exchange for agreeing to hold the hostages until after the election. (Some sources say former CIA Director George Bush and/or future CIA Director William Casey attended those meetings.)

October Surprise was also the name of a network of current and former CIA agents within Reagan's campaign whose job was to obtain intelligence from the Carter White House. It was a sophisticated—and ultimately successful—effort to destabilize the Carter administration.

The October Surprise team stole briefing books and other documents from the White House. They also leaked a series of fabricated stories to the media regarding Carter's negotiations with Iran and/or plans for a hostage rescue, which made both tasks considerably more difficult.

When Carter eventually did mount a hostage rescue, someone gave the Iranians—and William Casey—details about the operation in advance. It ended in disaster, with eight Americans dead.

Despite the October Surprise team's high-powered disinformation campaign, Carter managed to make a deal with the Iranians that didn't include trading arms for hostages (see Hit #34). But after the meeting in Paris, the Iranians backed out. The hostages weren't released until the very day of Reagan's inauguration—and millions of dollars in weaponry began flowing to Iran shortly thereafter.

The October Surprise deal has been subject to more disinformation and manipulation than any operation since the JFK assassination (Hit #9). Several key witnesses have met untimely deaths, as did one reporter who found links to other Reagan-era covert operations.

Finally, a Warren-Commission-type congressional investigation concluded that there was "no evidence" of a conspiracy. Unfortunately, there's plenty of evidence they never looked at, and there are several glaring errors in the report.

Hit #30: Libya

In April 1980, CIA agents Edwin Wilson and Frank Terpil were indicted for providing weapons and training to the regime of Libyan strongman Muamar al-Qadaffy. The CIA says that Terpil and Wilson were "rogue elephants" but Wilson, currently serving a life sentence in a federal penitentiary, claims he was acting under orders.

Wilson's claim is worth taking seriously. Many other members of the operation received slaps on the wrist and continued to work for the US government; some went on to be players in the Iran/contra scandal (Hit #34). The plastic explosives provided to Qadaffy may have been used in a number of bombings also connected to the CIA, including the assassination of Orlando Letelier (Hit #26).

Qadaffy has long enjoyed the status of official bogeyman to the US, firmly entrenched in this role while others like Noriega and Saddam have waxed and waned in it. Yet Qadaffy has also received weapons and training from the British and the Germans, and he's said to own 15% of the stock of Fiat, the largest company in Italy and a major defense contractor for the West.

The circumstances of Qadaffy's rise to power in a 1969 coup are also curious. Despite the vast amounts of oil wealth involved, Nixon and Kissinger lifted nary an eyebrow at Qadaffy's ouster of the pro-Western Libyan monarch. Immediately thereafter, Qadaffy began agitating for higher oil prices.

The Nixon administration announced that Qadaffy's suggested price hike was "justified" and the Shah of Iran (see Hit #3) agreed. The resulting surge in oil prices not only enriched the multinational oil companies but allowed the Shah to purchase billions in US arms, which he used to fulfill his role as regional policeman for the US.

If Qadaffy is actually a Western *agent provocateur*, it would hardly be unprecedented. Several radical Arab terrorists appear to be working both sides of the street (see Hit #35), while many other Arab heads of state have been on the CIA payroll.

But even if Qadaffy is just what he seems to be—a somewhat demented Arab nationalist—that still doesn't necessarily negate Wilson's claim. The CIA may have been infiltrating Qadaffy's regime in order to manipulate him for their own ends, and the operation may simply have blown up in their face (as have so many others).

Hit #31: Grenada

Here's what the US public was told: President Reagan woke up one day to discover that a horrible Marxist coup had taken over the Caribbean island of Grenada. Because there were Cuban troops on the island, the president had to send the US military to rescue US citizens trapped there and held as virtual hostages.

There was no way to get a more accurate picture, since the US military kept reporters from setting foot on Grenada during the invasion; a boatload of US journalists was turned away at gunpoint and all flights in and out were cancelled. Much later, long after everyone had stopped paying attention to Grenada, it became clear that the official story was built on a mountain of lies.

The CIA began destabilizing Grenada in 1979, when a man named Maurice Bishop (no relation to the spook mentioned in Hit #9) ousted the eccentric thug who ruled the island. Bishop set to work developing a better life for Grenada's citizens and earned much popular support for doing so. He ran afoul of the US fairly quickly, though, when he failed to join in the quarantine of Cuba.

Bishop's mildly socialist program (private enterprise left unmolested, but free health care, school lunches, etc.) was the final straw. Before long, a CIA propaganda campaign was portraying Grenada as a terrorist state allied to the Soviet Union, its 100,000 inhabitants armed to the teeth and poised to attack the pitifully vulnerable US.

The US invasion was planned at least two years before it happened, and CIA acts of sabotage proliferated. Money was given to opposition politicians and neighboring armies. Finally, in late 1983,

Bishop was overthrown by extremists in his own party and executed, and the US invasion began. CIA agents among the "hostages" helped coordinate the three-day war over shortwave radio.

As for the Cuban troops we invaded to protect our citizens from, there were 43 of them; the other Cubans on Grenada were mostly middle-aged construction workers. The Cubans let it be known that they would not interfere with the US "rescue," but the US troops fired on them and they defended themselves. That night, the US assured Cuba that its citizens in Grenada were "not a target"; the next day, we attacked them with helicopter gunships. When it was all over, 81 Cubans, 296 Grenadines and 131 Americans had been killed or wounded.

Today Grenada is back where it was before Bishop, mired in poverty and hopelessness. But, hey, it's no longer a threat to our very survival.

Hit #32: El Salvador

The fourteen families who rule El Salvador have never been squeamish about taking the life of anyone who gets in their way. Among the many people who commonly get in their way are the Catholic clergy, due to the concern they often show for the poor. As a result, a popular slogan among Salvadoran rightists is, "be patriotic—kill a priest."

In 1980, El Salvador's archbishop, Oscar Romero, made the mistake of taking President Carter's human rights rhetoric seriously. He wrote Carter, begging him to stop military support for El Salvador's murderous rulers. Carter ignored Romero, but the people who ran El Salvador didn't. Shortly after he sent the letter, Romero was shot through the heart while saying mass.

Romero's assassination was ordered by Roberto D'Aubuisson (daw-bwee-SAWN), nicknamed Blowtorch Bob for his favorite instrument of torture. A big admirer of Adolf Hitler, D'Aubuisson once said, "You Germans were very intelligent. You realized that the Jews were responsible for the spread of Communism and you began to kill them." D'Aubuisson has passed on, but his ARENA party, supported by the US, still rules El Salvador.

D'Aubuisson was a big wheel in the World Anti-Communist League. Organized in 1961, WACL serves as a worldwide umbrella organization for extreme-right militants. Among its members are expatriate Nazis, Italian terrorists, Japanese fascists, racist Afrikaners, Latin American death squad leaders and a number of US congressmen and "former" CIA agents.

Even aside from its participation in WACL, the CIA has done much to encourage bloodshed in El Salvador. With billions of dollars in US military aid at its disposal, it's flown air raids, waded into combat and trained the military units that formed the death squads.

The agency's spin doctors have also worked to improve the government's image. This often consisted of denying that atrocities like the 1982 massacre at El Mozote ever happened. Agency sycophants in the media parroted this line shamelessly until, in 1993, the UN Truth Commission investigated El Mozote and determined that 733 peasants had been murdered there. All in all, the Truth Commission concluded, 63,000 Salvadorans were killed between 1979 and 1992.

In 1982, after he was out of office, Jimmy Carter called El Salvador's government the "bloodthirstiest in the hemisphere." It's too bad he didn't come to that realization back when he—like his predecessors and successors—was funding it.

Hit #33: Nicaragua

FDR once remarked of Nicaragua's dictator, "Somoza may be a son of a bitch, but he's *our* son of a bitch." So when a later Somoza (the son of our son of a bitch) was overthrown in 1979, we spared no effort until Nicaragua was ours again.

When President Carter saw that the younger Somoza's days were numbered, he tried to ease him out of power, unaware that retired CIA agents were providing him with further weaponry. Carter's plan was to keep Somoza's private army, the National Guard, in power, while Somoza escaped to enjoy his $900-million fortune.

Most Nicaraguans, having suffered 46 years of the Guard's unrelenting brutality, were not thrilled with that plan. When Somoza fell, so did his hated National Guard.

Many of the Guard were evacuated on US planes. We reassambled them, armed and supplied them, had them trained by Argentinian death squads and sent them back to harass the new regime. Because the Guard was so despised in Nicaragua, they were given a new name—the *contras* (an abbreviation of the Spanish word for *counter-revolutionaries)*.

The resulting bloodshed was perhaps the least covert of all CIA covert operations. President Reagan was perfectly candid about the goals—the second-poorest nation in the hemisphere was to be "pressured" until "they say 'uncle'."

The methods became part of the public record too—though not intentionally—when the CIA's *Freedom Fighters Manual* was leaked to the press. It gave detailed instructions on assassination, sabotage, kidnapping, blackmail and the slaughter of civilians.

The US lavished military and financial aid on the contras, whom they used to terrorize rural Nicaragua. Since many peasants were delighted that the new government was providing them with teachers and doctors (for the first time ever), the contras particularly targeted those professionals.

The CIA mined harbors and blew up fuel tanks, then told the contras to claim credit. The agency flew supplies to the contras, attempted to assassinate the Nicaraguan leadership and pumped millions of dollars into opposition politicians. And, as in Chile, they made the economy "scream" (see Hit #17).

Finally, in 1989, after ten years of warfare—both economic and military—the Nicaraguans gave up and voted for the US-backed slate of candidates. If any of them wondered what would happen should they fail to do so, they only needed to look south to Panama, which had just been invaded by the US the month before (see Hit #39).

Hit #34: Iran/contra

The Reagan administration brought out the worst in the CIA—its tendency to distort intelligence to justify policies, its fanatical enthusiasm for covert action and its disdain for congressional oversight. Reagan's CIA director, William Casey, was running so many off-the-books operations that he gutted the agency's counterintelligence division out of fear that it would find out what he was up to. This made it absurdly easy for moles and traitors to continue operating, and led to an embarrassing series of spy scandals that continue to this day.

The most famous of these was Iran/contra, which began with a series of arms deals with the Muslim theocracy of Iran. The weapons shipments began in March 1981, years before there were any new hostages to trade arms for. This lends credence to the theory that the arms were actually a payoff for the October Surprise deal (Hit #29).

Oliver North and his cronies charged the Iranians ridiculously high mark-ups on the weapons they sold them, and some profits from this were used to buy arms for the Nicaraguan contras (see Hit #33), in blatant defiance of a Congressional ban. (Actually, more of the money ended up in private bank accounts than ever reached the contras.)

All CIA covert actions are supposed to be authorized by a presidential "finding," but Iran/contra ran for years without one. Once the participants realized they were committing impeachable offenses, they had the president sign a "retroactive finding." It was later destroyed, to protect Reagan.

Because the half-hearted Congressional probe into Iran/contra had secretly agreed in advance to avoid any evidence that might lead to Reagan's impeachment, it hardly scratched the surface. For example, it barely touched on the CIA's involvement in contra drug trafficking (see Hit #22), nor did it delve into covert manipulation of US elections with a variety of secret funds—even though several US representatives opposed to the contra war were defeated as a result of it.

The Iran/contra operation set up something called the Office of Public Diplomacy, which used taxpayers' own money to convince them that the CIA's secret wars were a great idea. (This was really just an aboveground example of the CIA's normal propaganda efforts, as described in Hit #24.)

Probably the most dangerous part of the whole Iran/contra mess was Oliver North's draft of a plan to suspend the US Constitution in case of anti-war protests. One Congressman tried to ask about this, but was gaveled down and told it could be only discussed in "executive session."

Hit #35: Pan Am Flight 103

Syrian terrorist Monzer al-Kassar had a great set-up. He ran a Frankfurt-to-New York heroin smuggling operation that netted him millions, and the whole thing was protected by the CIA. This was payback for serving as a middleman in Oliver North's Iran/contra deals (see Hit #34) and also in the hope that he'd use his influence to secure the release of US hostages in Beirut. Al-Kassar's accomplice at the Frankfurt airport regularly substituted a suitcase full of heroin for an identical suitcase checked onto a Pan Am flight to New York.

Major Charles McKee, a CIA agent charged with rescuing US hostages in Beirut, was outraged when he heard of the smuggling operation, and felt it could jeopardize his mission. He complained bitterly to the CIA, but got only silence in reply. Impulsively, and against CIA procedures, McKee and four other members of his team decided to fly home and expose the deal with al-Kassar. Their flight connected with Pan Am Flight 103 in London.

On December 20, 1989, a German government agent in Frankfurt who was privy to the heroin deal noticed that the switched suitcase being put onto Pan Am Flight 103 looked completely different than it usually did. Aware that a bomb threat had been made against the flight, he called his local CIA contact and asked what was up. "Don't worry about it," he was told. "Don't stop it. Let it go."

When Flight 103 left London, not only was the McKee team on board, but also a US Justice department Nazi hunter and a UN diplomat mediating conflicts in southern Africa. South Africa's foreign minister was booked on the flight as well, but luckily cancelled at the last minute.

When the plane blew up over Lockerbie, Scotland, killing 270 people, a team of CIA agents was on their way to the wreckage within the hour. Disguised as Pan Am employees, they removed evidence from the crash site, then later returned it (or something similar) to be rediscovered.

Initial investigations focused on Syria and Iran, with the possible motive being revenge for an Iranian plane shot down by a US warship the previous July. But when Syria's cooperation was needed during the Gulf War, the blame was shifted to our favorite whipping boy, Libya (see Hit #30).

Pan Am conducted its own investigation, which uncovered the links to al-Kassar. But it was unable to secure CIA documents on the case, and lost a massive lawsuit filed by the families of Flight 103 victims. Soon after, it filed for bankruptcy.

Hit #36: Afghanistan

During the Reagan years, the CIA ran nearly two dozen covert operations against various governments. Of these, Afghanistan was by far the biggest; it was, in fact, the biggest CIA operation of all time, both in terms of dollars spent ($5–$6 billion) and personnel involved. Yet it not only generated little controversy, but enjoyed strong bipartisan support. That's because its main purpose was to "bleed" the Soviet Union, just as we had been bled in Vietnam.

Prior to the 1979 Russian invasion, Afghanistan was ruled by a brutal dictator. Like the neighboring Shah of Iran, he allowed the CIA to set up radar installations in his country that were used to monitor the Soviets. In 1979, after several dozen Soviet advisors were massacred by Afghan tribesmen, the USSR sent in the Red Army.

The Soviets tried to install a pliable client regime, without taking local attitudes much into account. Many of the mullahs who controlled chunks of Afghan territory objected to Soviet efforts to educate women and to institute land reform. Others, outraged by the USSR's attempts to suppress the heroin trade, shifted their operations to Pakistan (see Hit #22).

As for the CIA, its aim was simply to humiliate the Soviets by arming anyone who would fight against them. The agency funnelled cash and weapons to over a dozen guerrilla groups, many of whom had been staging raids from Pakistan years before the Soviet invasion. Today, long after the Soviet Union left Afghanistan (and, in fact, has ceased to exist), most of these groups are still fighting each other for control of the country.

Besides tossing billions of dollars into the conflict, the CIA transferred sensitive weapons technology to fanatical Muslim extremists, with consequences that will haunt the US for years to come. One notable veteran of the Afghan operation is Sheik Abdel Rahman, famous for his role in the World Trade Center bombing.

The CIA succeeded in creating chaos, but never developed a plan for *ending* it. When the ten-year war was over, a million people were dead, and Afghan heroin had captured 60% of the US market.

Hit #37: South Pacific

In 1993, US citizens were shocked to learn that their government had performed nuclear experiments on innocent and unknowing test subjects. To the residents of US-administered "trust territories" in the South Pacific, this was an old story.

Ever since we nuked Japan in August 1945, the US had regarded the Pacific as an "American lake." For years, both the US and France tested nuclear weapons and lobbed missiles at various Pacific islands under their "trusteeship," hustling the natives out of the way.

Sometimes natives were returned prematurely to their irradiated homelands, which resulted in birth defects and cancers. Not surprisingly, this led to particularly strong anti-nuclear sentiments among the Pacific islanders. Also not surprisingly, the CIA has done everything in its power to counter them.

The US has occupied the tiny island of Belau since World War II and, despite native calls for self-determination, is unlikely to depart anytime soon. In 1979, the Belauans had the effrontery to pass the world's first anti-nuclear constitution.

Since then, the US has sponsored *ten* elections in an unsuccessful effort to revise the document. Because the Pentagon wants to keep a military base on Belau for the next 30 years or so, there have been endless beatings and assassinations of Belauan anti-nuclear activists.

The island nation of Kanaky (also known as New Caledonia) has been occupied by French troops since a bogus 1987 election that "ratified" French rule. Kanaky's exiled resistance movement receives support from the island nation of Vanuatu (formerly called New Hebrides), which has one of the most progressive governments in the Pacific. The CIA has been funnelling money into destabilizing Vanuatu, which it charges is the victim of "Libyan subversion."

In Fiji, a pro-US government was replaced by a progressive coalition in a 1987 election; less than a month later, a CIA-backed coup deposed the elected government. CIA "coup experts," including the head of the World Anti-Communist League (see Hit #32), were on hand before, during and after the coup. The new ruling junta purchased US helicopters to use against any Fijians who have the gall to imagine they have the right to elect whomever they please.

Hit #38: Crooked Banks

Since British bank examiners first shut down its London branch in 1991, BCCI (the Bank of Credit and Commerce International) has become known as "the world's crookedest bank"—or, as CIA Director Robert Gates called it, the Bank of Crooks and Criminals International. He, of all people, should know.

Throughout its entire history, the CIA has set up an elaborate shell game of "proprietaries" (front companies), money-laundering operations and off-the-books projects so complex that no outsider—and few insiders—could ever keep track of them. BCCI was neither the first nor the last of these.

An important predecessor was the Nugan Hand Bank (see Hit #22), which helped the CIA topple a pesky government in its host country, Australia. Capitalized with booty from drug and weapons deals in the last years of the Vietnam War, it helped finance agency operations in Angola and the Middle East.

Nugan Hand's board was loaded with spooks, including former CIA Director William Colby. When Australian bank examiners closed in on the bank in 1977, Nugan killed himself and Hand disappeared with billions in depositors' funds.

The CIA flirted with a similar operation in Hawaii, but eventually chose the Pakistan-based BCCI. It welcomed anyone with large amounts of cash to launder, from narcotics traffickers to arms merchants, terrorists to gangster governments.

Naturally, the CIA felt right at home. In fact, one former BCCI official claims to have been told that the CIA, and Director Richard Helms in particular, actually started the bank, and that it "wasn't a Pakistani bank at all."

Before collapsing, BCCI managed to facilitate a host of CIA covert operations, notably George Bush's efforts to pump weapons to Saddam Hussein's Iraq (see Hit #40) and Edwin Wilson's "unauthorized" arming of Libya (see Hit #30).

Efforts to unravel all of BCCI's mysteries will never succeed. Its directors had the good sense to feather the nests of enough prominent US politicians, of both parties, to ensure that any investigation will be half-hearted at best.

Not surprisingly, CIA-connected lobbyists have worked to undermine any probe. Roughly $20 billion of BCCI's assets remain unaccounted for.

Hit #39: Panama

For most of his life, Manuel Noriega got along very well with the CIA. As far back as 1959, he was reporting on Panamanian leftists to the Americans; by 1966, he was on the CIA payroll. Despite—or maybe because of—Noriega's "perverse" treatment of prisoners, he was deemed worthy to be trained at the notorious School of the Americas (also known as the "School of Dictators" or the "School of Assassins"), run by the US Army in Panama City (it's since moved to Ft. Benning, Georgia).

As early as 1972, reports of Noriega's drug trafficking irked the DEA, and the State Department complained of his dealings with other intelligence services, notably those of Israel and Cuba. Don't worry, said the CIA—he's our boy.

In 1976, Noriega paid a visit to CIA Director George Bush in Washington. Bush's successor was less comfortable with Noriega and took him off the CIA payroll, but when Bush became vice-president in 1980, Noriega went back on, with a six-figure annual salary.

In 1981, Panama's popular head of state, Omar Torrijos, was killed in a plane crash; by 1983, Noriega had consolidated his control. In 1987, a close Noriega aide corroborated what many suspected—Noriega had sabotaged Torrijos' plane. (The CIA has also been linked to the assassination, in 1955, of Panama's president, allegedly with the approval of then-Vice-President Nixon).

Nothing Noriega did seemed to upset the CIA. If he smuggled cocaine on contra supply planes (see Hits #22, 33 & 34)...well, he wasn't the only one. If he beheaded a political opponent who accused him of drug running...well, he was just being firm.

If he used violence and fraud to steal the 1984 Panamanian elections...well, we couldn't have been more pleased with the outcome.

By 1989, however, the love affair was over. Noriega had angered his handlers by waffling on his opposition to the Sandinistas in Nicaragua and he was showing other disquieting signs of disobedience. In December 1989, US troops invaded Panama to "arrest" Noriega, slaughtering 2,000–4,000 innocent civilians in the process.

What changed after the invasion? Violence, fraud and drug trafficking continued unabated. But, unlike Noriega, Panama's new rulers knew how to follow orders, and agreed to reconsider the Torrijos treaties, under which all US military bases in Panama would be shut down by the year 2000. (In 1994, Torrijos' and Noriega's old party was voted back in—so look for more CIA sabotage.)

Hit #40: Iraq

The Gulf War of early 1991 didn't change much. Our old buddy, the despotic Emir of Kuwait, is back on his throne. Our former buddy, Saddam Hussein, while knocked down a peg or two, is still in power and as brutal as ever. Hundreds of thousands of Iraqis are dead, hundreds of US veterans are suffering from a mysterious disease, and the Persian Gulf has been ravaged by the largest oil spill in history. The question naturally arises, could any of this have been avoided?

The whole dispute started because Kuwait was slant-drilling. Using equipment bought from National Security Council chief Brent Scowcroft's old company, Kuwait was pumping out some $14-billion worth of oil from underneath Iraqi territory. Even the territory they were drilling *from* had originally been Iraq's. Slant-drilling is enough to get you shot in Texas, and it's certainly enough to start a war in the Mideast.

Even so, this dispute could have been negotiated. But it's hard to *avoid* a war when what you're actually doing is trying to *provoke* a war.

The most famous example of that is the meeting between Saddam and the US Ambassador to Iraq, April Glaspie, five days before Iraq invaded Kuwait. As CIA satellite photos showed an Iraqi invasion force massing on the Kuwaiti border, Glaspie told Hussein that "the US takes no position" on Iraq's dispute with Kuwait.

A few days later, during last-minute negotiations, Kuwait's foreign minister said: "We are not going to respond to [Iraq]....If they don't like it, let them occupy our territory....We are going to bring in the Americans." The US reportedly encouraged Kuwait's attitude.

Pitting the two countries against each other was nothing new. Back in 1989, CIA Director William Webster advised Kuwait's security chief to "take advantage of the deteriorating economic situation in Iraq...to put pressure on [Iraq]." At the same time, a CIA-linked think tank was advising Saddam to put pressure on the Kuwaitis.

A month earlier, the Bush administration issued a secret directive that called for greater economic cooperation with Iraq. This ultimately resulted in billions of dollars of illegal arms sales to Saddam.

The Gulf War further destabilized the region and made Kuwait more dependent on us. US oil companies can now exert more control over oil prices (and thus boost their profits). The US military got an excuse to build more bases in the region (which Saudi Arabia, for one, didn't want) and the war also helped justify the "need" to continue exorbitant levels of military spending. Finally, it sent a message to Third World leaders about what they could expect if they dared to step out of line.

Hit #41: Haiti

US troops invaded Haiti five times, once staying for almost twenty years (1915–35). At the end of that prolonged visit, during which we killed thousands of Haitians for daring to rebel, we left the country in the hands of the local National Guard, confident that they'd carry on our good work.

From this arrangement emerged the Duvalier family dynasty and their private terrorist force, the machete-wielding Tontons Macoutes. "Papa Doc" Duvalier (he was a medical doctor) also relied on voodoo incantations and, during a 1959 uprising, the timely assistance of the US military. When Papa Doc died in 1971, his 19-year-old son, called Baby Doc, became "president-for-life."

Throughout the blood-drenched rule of the Duvaliers (nearly 100,000 killed by the Tontons Macoutes alone), the US barely uttered a peep about human rights violations. In 1986, however, when it became apparent that Baby Doc's presidency could not in fact be sustained for his entire life (unless he died soon), the Reagan administration airlifted him to a retirement villa in France and started talking about the "democratic process."

Before that could begin, however, the Haitian military had to be further strengthened. CIA money began flowing to Haiti, which had already seen US aid double during the Reagan years. The CIA set up an antinarcotics service called—appropriately—SIN ("national intelligence service"). As one CIA man admitted, SIN used its millions in CIA subsidies mainly to suppress popular movements by means of torture and assassination. Far from combatting drugs, many SIN officers engage in the drug trade themselves.

In 1990, elections were finally allowed. Haitians stunned the US by rejecting the candidate we preferred in favor of a left-wing Catholic priest, Jean-Bertrand Aristide. The Bush administration could scarcely conceal its joy when Haiti's US-trained military deposed Aristide eight months later.

When Bill Clinton took office, he offered lip service to the idea of returning Aristide to power. Even this hypocritical posturing was too much for the CIA, who leaked a "psychological profile" that painted the courageous, dedicated Aristide as a "psychopath."

Endless waves of refugees, and US embarrassment over more than 4,000 killings by Haitian security forces, have led to even more vigorous US lip service. But if history is any indication, the chances of a government coming to power that meets the needs of the Haitian people are slim to none.

Hit #42 : *Yugoslavia*

The bloodshed and chaos that have engulfed Yugoslavia since its breakup have been portrayed as the inevitable result of bottled-up ethnic tensions. But there's considerable evidence that both the breakup and the warfare were encouraged by Western intelligence services—including Germany's BND, the successor to the Gehlen Org (see Hit #1).

Germany's interests in the region date to World War II, when the Bosnians and Croats allied with the Nazis against the Serbs, who the Nazis regarded as *untermenschen* (subhumans). After Germany reunified in 1989, it began to take a more expansionist attitude toward Eastern Europe, and Yugoslavia in particular. In 1990, it urged the Bush administration to help it dismantle Yugoslavia.

Bush was happy to comply, since the US had longstanding plans to overthrow Yugoslavia's government. Yugoslavia had recently renounced the market-oriented "shock treatment" prescribed for it, which had been causing social unrest, so it was a prime candidate for further destabilization.

The Germans encouraged Croatia to secede from Yugoslavia, and Bosnia soon followed. Germany immediately recognized the new nations, forcing the hand of the European Community, which had wanted to take a more cautious approach. The new Croatian state adopted the flag and anthem of its WWII Nazi puppet regime—and, in some cases, the same personnel.

Virulently fascist Croats had long been active in the World Anti-Communist League (see Hit #32) and other exile groups nurtured by the CIA. Many Eastern European Nazis had gone on to work with the CIA, either in the US or in covert operations abroad. With the collapse of Communism in Eastern Europe, many of these aging chickens came home to roost. Neofascist movements are active in Lithuania, Hungary and Romania, as well as in much of Western Europe (notably Italy).

Despite an official arms embargo against Croatia and Bosnia, Western powers immediately began covertly arming them, which would have been impossible without the knowledge and acquiescence of the CIA and the BND. Mercenaries from Britain, Germany and the US are said to be serving alongside the Croat militias—a sure sign of an ongoing covert operation. In fact, in 1994, the CIA opened a new base in Albania to monitor troop movements and "potential targets."

Sources

I relied on two sources more than others: William Blum's indispensible overview *The CIA: A Forgotten History* (Zed Books, 1986), referred to below simply as Blum, and the past fifteen years of *Covert Action Information Bulletin,* a vital periodical now known simply as *Covert Action (*1500 Massachusetts Ave NW, #732, Washington DC 20005), referred to below as *CAIB.*

Mark Zepezauer

Hit #1: E.H. Cookridge, *Gehlen: Spy of the Century,* Random House, 1971; Carl Oglesby, "The Secret Treaty of Fort Hunt," *CAIB* #35 (Fall 1990); Charles Higham, *Trading With the Enemy,* Delacorte, 1983; Ladislas Farago, *Aftermath,* Avon, 1974. **Hit #2:** Warren Hinckle, "The CIA's 'secret army' activity in Italy," *San Francisco Examiner,* 11/22/90; Patrice Claude, "Strange tale of terrorism, sabotage shakes Italy," *San Francisco Chronicle,* 11/14/90; William Scobie, "Secret army's war on the left," *London Observer,* 11/18/90. **Hit #3:** Blum, Ch. 9. **Hit #4:** Stephen Kinzer, *Bitter Fruit: The Untold Story of the American Coup in Guatemala,* Anchor, 1983; Blum, Ch. 10. **Hit #5:** Walter Bowart, *Operation Mind Control,* Dell, 1978; John Marks, *The Search for the Manchurian Candidate,* Dell, 1979. **Hit #6:** Blum, Ch. 26 & 42. **Hit #7:** Michael Beschloss, *Mayday: Eisenhower, Khrushchev and the U-2 Affair,* Harper & Row, 1986; Fletcher Prouty, *JFK: The CIA, Vietnam and the Plot to Assassinate John F. Kennedy,* Birch Lane, 1992. **Hit #8:** Warren Hinckle & William Turner, *Deadly Secrets: The CIA-Mafia War Against Castro and the Assassination of JFK,* Thunder's Mouth, 1992; Blum, Ch. 30. **Hit #9:** Philip Melanson, *Spy Saga: Lee Harvey Oswald and US Intelligence,* Praeger, 1990; Jim Marrs, *Crossfire: The Plot That Killed Kennedy,* Carroll & Graf, 1989. **Hit #10:** Marilyn B. Young, *The Vietnam Wars 1945–1990,* Harper Perennial, 1991. **Hit #11:** Blum, Ch. 29. **Hit #12:** Karl Evanzz, *The Judas Factor: The Plot to Kill Malcolm X,* Thunder's Mouth, 1992. **Hit #13:** Blum, Ch. 14 & 31. **Hit #14:** Blum, Ch. 3 & 35. **Hit #15**: Philip Melanson, *Who Killed Martin Luther King?,* Odonian, 1993; *CAIB* #34 (Summer 1990). **Hit #16:** Philip Melanson, *Who Killed Robert Kennedy?,* Odonian, 1993; William Turner & Jonn Christian, *The Assassination of Robert F. Kennedy,* Thunder's Mouth, 1993; Robert Morrow, *The Senator Must Die,* Roundtable, 1988. **Hit #17:** Blum, Ch. 34. **Hit #18:** Young (see Hit #10); Blum, Ch. 19. **Hit #19:** William Shawcross, *Sideshow: Nixon, Kissinger and the Destruction of Cambodia,* Simon and Schuster, 1979; Blum, Ch. 20. **Hit #20:** Blum, Ch. 21. **Hit #21:** Verne Lyon, "The History of Operation CHAOS," *CAIB* #34 (Summer 1990). **Hit #22:** Alfred McCoy, *The Politics of*

Heroin in Southeast Asia, Harper Colophon, 1973; Peter Dale Scott & Jonathan Marshall, *Cocaine Politics*, University of California, 1992. **Hit #23:** Jim Hougan, *Secret Agenda: Watergate, Deep Throat and the CIA*, Random House, 1984; Deborah Davis, *Katherine the Great: Katherine Graham and the Washington Post*, Harcourt Brace Jovanovitch, 1979; Len Colodny & Robert Gettelin, *Silent Coup: The Removal of a President*, St. Martins, 1991. **Hit #24:** Carl Bernstein, "The CIA and the Media," *Rolling Stone*, 10/20/77. **Hit #25:** John Stockwell, *In Search of Enemies*, Norton, 1978; Blum, Ch. 41. **Hit #26:** Donald Freed & Fred Landis, *Death in Washington: The Murder of Orlando Letelier*, Laurence Hill, 1980. **Hit #27:** Mark Perry, *The Last Days of the CIA*, Wm. Morrow, 1992. **Hit #28:** John Judge, "The Black Hole of Guyana," in *Secret and Suppressed*, edited by Jim Keith, Feral House, 1993. **Hit #29:** Barbara Honneger, *October Surprise*, Tudor, 1989; Robert Parry, *Trick or Treason*, Sheridan Square, 1993. **Hit #30:** Jack Anderson, *Fiasco*, Times Books, 1983; John M. Blair, *The Control of Oil*, Vintage Books, 1976; Peter Maas, *Manhunt*, Random House, 1986. George Tremlett, *Gadaffi: The Desert Mystic*, Carroll & Graf, 1993. **Hit #31:** Ellen Ray & Bill Schaap, "US Crushes Caribbean Jewel," *CAIB* #20 (Winter 1984); Blum, Ch. 45. **Hit #32:** Blum, Ch. 48; Scott & Jon Lee Anderson, *Inside the League*, Dodd, Mead, 1986. Raymond Bonner, *Weakness and Deceit*, Times Books, 1984. **Hit #33:** Peter Kornbluh, *Nicaragua: The Price of Intervention*, IPS, 1987; Leslie Cockburn, *Out of Control*, Atlantic Monthly Press, 1987. **Hit #34:** Theodore Draper, *A Very Thin Line*, Hill and Wang, 1991; Doug Vaughn, "Walsh's Final Iran-Contra Report," *CAIB* #48, (Spring 1994). **Hit #35:** Maggie Mahar, "Unwitting Accomplices?," *Barrons*, 12/17/90, Roy Rowan, "Pan Am 103: Why Did They Die?" *Time*, 4/27/92; Jeff Jones, "The Bombing of Pan Am 103," *CAIB* #34 (Summer 1990). **Hit #36:** "Under the Bush with the CIA" (interview with John Stockwell), *Z Magazine*, September 1989. **Hit #37:** Glen Alcalay, "Bombed, robbed, relocated, irradiated by US, France," *National Guardian (US)*, 11/25/87; *CAIB* #29 (Winter 1988). **Hit #38:** Jonathan Kwitny, *The Crimes of Patriots*, Touchstone Books, 1988; Mark Potts, *Dirty Money: The World's Sleaziest Bank*, National Press, 1992; Jack Calhoun, "BCCI: Bank of the CIA," *CAIB* #44 (Spring 1993). *Newsweek*, 12/7/92. **Hit #39:** Independent Commission of Inquiry on the US Invasion of Panama, *The US Invasion of Panama: The Truth behind Operation "Just Cause,"* South End, 1991. **Hit #40:** Ramsey Clark, *The Fire This Time: US War Crimes in the Gulf*, Thunder's Mouth, 1992. **Hit #41:** John Canham-Clyde, "Haiti: Selling Out Democracy," *CAIB* #48 (Spring 1994). **Hit #42:** Sean Gervasi, "Germany, US and the Yugoslavia Crisis," *CAIB* #43 (Winter 1992–93).

Index

WHAT UNCLE SAM REALLY WANTS
NOAM CHOMSKY

A brilliant look at the real motivations behind US foreign policy, from the man the *New York Times* called "arguably the most important intellectual alive." 111 pp. $8.50. *Highly recommended. —Booklist*

216,000 copies in print

❦

THE PROSPEROUS FEW
AND THE RESTLESS MANY   NOAM CHOMSKY

This wide-ranging state-of-the-world report offers Chomsky's pentrating insights on everything from Bosnia to biotechnology. 95 pp. $8.

Calmly reasoned. Most welcome. –Newsday

142,000 copies in print

❦

SECRETS, LIES AND DEMOCRACY
NOAM CHOMSKY

The third in Chomsky's series of state-of-the-world reports, this fascinating book concludes with a list of organizations worth putting time and effort into. 127 pp. $9.

123,000 copies in print

❦

THE COMMON GOOD   NOAM CHOMSKY

This illusion-shattering masterpiece discusses Aristotle, the US left and everything in between. 191 pp. $12.   **47,000 copies in print**

❦

EAST TIMOR: GENOCIDE IN PARADISE
2nd edition   MATTHEW JARDINE
INTRODUCTION BY NOAM CHOMSKY

Chomsky calls it "perhaps the greatest death toll relative to the population since the Holocaust." The US supported the genocide. 95 pp. $8.